BEND

Natasha Sajé

Salt Lake City
February 2004

Natasha Sajé

BEND

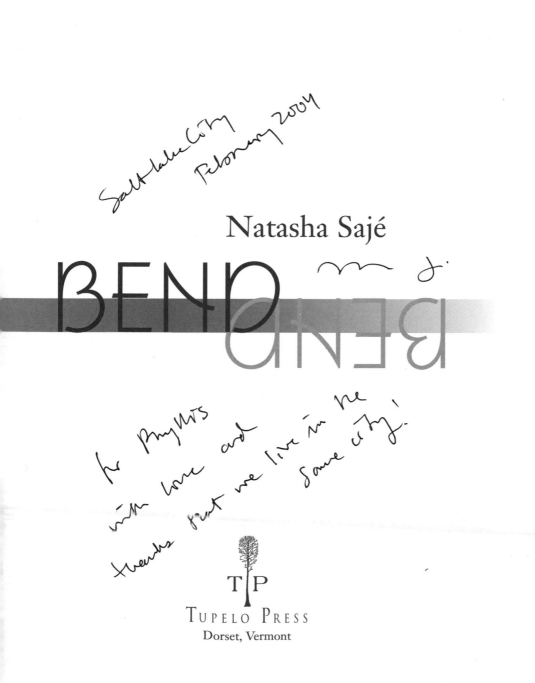

for Phyllis
with love and
thanks that we live in the
same city!

T|P

TUPELO PRESS
Dorset, Vermont

First paperback edition January, 2004
Library of Congress Control Number: 2003104719
Tupelo Press
PO Box 539, Dorset, Vermont 05251
802.366.8185 • Fax 802.362.1883
editor@tupelopress.org • web www.tupelopress.org

Cover art: Gustave Courbet, *The Mediterranean*, 1857 The Phillips Collection, Washington, D.C.
Cover and text designed by William Kuch, WK Graphic Design

for Tyrone Robertson

Contents

A Minor Riot at the Mint -1

A Minor Riot at the Mint

Custome is the most certain Mistresse of language, as the publicke stampe makes current money. But we must not be too frequent with the mint, every day coyning.
—Ben Jonson

Into my pocket slips a folded note, creased
like labia, cached with private promise.
Pea blossoms in broth. And my *in petto*
pleasure in thinking the missive
for me, the edges keen against
my thumb, my plotting to be alone and open it.
Is it tame as a Hepplewhite chair
or nubile as a pitchfork?

The ship rolls through open water,
dirty in the bay around Rio.
I'm a crazy sailor on the gravy boat,
a woman of means. This letter's mine only
till St. Geoffrey's Day, and if
the paper degrades, that's how it goes
with money. I'll wave the wealth
where any frigate bird can snatch it.

O my mackintosh,
my bilbo, my cistern, my confiture,

I love you so much you breathe me away.

**Reading Henry Fowler's *Modern English Usage*
in Salt Lake City in November**

You note the one "r" in iridescent,
from the Greek, *iris*, rainbow, not the Latin,
irrideo, to laugh, and I smile

to think of your idiosyncrasy,
scrupulous care in life as well as work.
Today light streams in, the bright surprise

of it risible, as amazing to me
as sagebrush and piñons. First Western fall,
felicitous, pumpkin custard sending

clove into the air as the cats quibble
over the patch of hottest sun. Gone:
Old house, old roads, old friends. Gone as well

that blue hour when solitary
lovers in cafés console themselves.
That city's farther than it's ever been,

differs *toto caelo*, by the whole sky,
from these nights of shooting stars
and sunny days that beam across the floor

like lace. If you were here, Henry,
you'd advise exactitude, tell me to love
the narrow difference between "broad"

and "wide": a distance that separates
the limits, an amplitude of what
connects them. Some words refuse wide,

admit broad: blade, spearhead, daylight.
And some allow them both: A wide door
open to miles of snowy peaks. The view

from where I am is wide *and* broad, and if
I lose myself in its expanse, will mountains
rein me in, or clouds volatile as grace?

In the Garden

Bend
       and make the horizon disappear.

      Desire's a hardy trifoliate
               orange with thorns:

        viscous bitter fluid, flesh crammed
          full of seeds.

            Heavenly florid citrus scent.

Marigolds in neat rows
       in a garden as tangled as the arms

          of an orange bush.

Feet are not straight.
Belly is not.

        They curve like hills
    covered with gentian blooming deep night blue,
      the color of September at eight o'clock,
        summer's final   pulse.

        Bend
           and make the horizon disappear
           from a narrow place
where the sea rushes
      between two spits of land

      from one aqueous

        body to another.

Fruit

Pitting a flat of sour cherries squeezing fingers through crisp skins takes all day thinking silly mind games and how the still life makes me happy even though the light is fading and someone's stolen the marigolds out front and maybe that's why I spend six hours finding pits in order to throw them out betting on whether I've got the last one and if I do then I will be loved and if not I'll be loved by someone else.

Heloise to Abelard

If you were here, my love,
I would tear the pages of my books,

pleat them into baskets for collecting cherries,
the kind that do not bleed.

I would strip the bark from birches
and build a coffin for our fears—

clouds would carry it to Rome.
I would turn into a river fluke

to enter the soft soles of your feet.
And I would lie with you

on the stone floor of the chapel,
morning light filtering through panes.

My love, if you were here,
you would fog the cold surface

of my soul with your breath,
and I would turn to you

and say, *if you were not
here, Heloise would be writing.*

Wonders of the Invisible World

Muses are no better than harlots
                            —Cotton Mather, 1726

Strange that he mentions muses.
Demons, yes. God, of course.
But harlots? Perhaps

in his last year, nearly
destitute, having out-lived
thirteen of his children,

the doctor of divinity—this man
who once wrote in his diary
about the wife who almost killed

him with her madness, *Misera*
mea conjux in *Paroxysmos*
illos vere Satanicos—felt

another sorceress nuzzling
his ears about the price of flesh
before spinning it into words,

and he knew that she too would leave
him bereft of a sweet and wicked
sustenance. Or perhaps he remembered

thirty years before, the *Time of the Devils*
coming down in great Wrath,
too many Tongues and Hearts

set on fire of Hell,
and imagined a world pervaded
by a cutting yellow wind

with wraithlike women moving
soul to soul, streaming like water
off a roof, flooding the mouth of every man

who had ever meant to hang them.

Welcome, Reader

to the cellar where you'll be pointed
at the cement ceiling and its drips of condensation.
How will they tumble, each unpredictable drop?

A whole cloud of philosophy condensed
into a drop of grammar. Will you think of me
in my sunny kitchen with its pots of basil

and rosemary, baking blueberry crisp, opening the door
now and then to let the scent waft down? Or napping
under a comforter, dreaming of you? No, reader,

because if you're in the basement, so am I,
and we'll have Wittgenstein: *the world is everything*
that is the case: everything is, as it were, in a space

of possible atomic facts. Think of the space as empty
but not of the thing without the space. That'll make time
crawl, our sentence a sentence, a term hard

to change. We'll be the Houdinis of our quaint bunker,
and the deeper we go, the more the pleasure of digging
will be its own reward, pleasantly tired arms, not the glow

of China in the distance. *The limits of our language mean*
the limits of our world. Sure it'd be easier to live in a
shore house built on pylons of treated lumber,

but who wants air underfoot? Trust me, soon
the rooms upstairs will seem garish, department store
aisles filled with everything we don't need.

Between the Lines

Devil's thorn, wormleaf, itchgrass, witchweed, broomrape—
words can cover acres. I want to mow them
down, plug my ears with cotton, enjoy the weeds
already buried within. Sleep taking
place in a hush of sand. Some words are heard
through the rubble of a burnt-out city, the noise of bombs.
Think of a mother hearing her child fall silent
in another room, that evil quiet. Think of how the Pope
remained silent when he could have spoken.
An American girl in 1915 would write
on pages the color of pigeon's blood, with white ink,
a curious fashion like **ALGERIAN** font today.
What difference does the instrument make? Less
than the difference between pouring and spilling. Truth
jettisoned off the side of a ship moving through
clouds of weeds. The problem of the non-
indigenous, their invasive nature. Who
can speak for the past? The motif here
is eradication. *Open the archives!*

White

Seeing is forgetting the name of the thing one sees.
—Paul Valéry

In the air a pen moves
over a milk-white field lined faint green,
and a pair of eyes reads
the long "y's," straight "I's,"
"a's" with mouths open like birds
hungry for worms. Bent within the lines,
each curved letter is marked into place,
a gravestone falling into its row.
The dark road under the snow,
the heart's pulse hammering
at wrists and neck.

One has to remain very still to see.
    One has to remain still.

The hand unfurls laundry on a line,
waits for sun to dry and bleach it,
for someone to take it
down, for anyone to wear it.
Wind blows the cloth off the line
or rain soaks and freezes the cloth,
dragging and breaking the cord,
coming to rest in a field.

In a field. Coming to rest.

                    Where does one stand to see
the sheets and small briefs fluttering
or frozen, in a landscape
transformed by weather, themselves
transformed
                    by weather?

I See

the cats playing with a rose fallen
from a wreath: a stiff silvery stem

topped by a dark pink ball.
How curiously they bat the rose,

sniffing it with glee, and that's what
makes me bend, and see that it's really

the long dried tail and entrails of a rat.
I laugh: If rose & rat are not so far

apart, then what can't be mistaken
for something that it's not?

The turn's a way of telling me
to make each breath a self-revision.

Wave

A few memories float—
two orange cats entwined on the green armchair,
birthday lunch with my mother in the department store tearoom
when women still wore hats and white gloves—
but most are lost. An only child,
center of her parents' world, whose childhood
seems to have disappeared, except when wind
churns up a shell: the spring I had measles
and lay outside wrapped in blankets,
reading. My parents' stories, always the same ones:
I never asked for anything, I wouldn't
eat what they prepared. Someone said childhood
would be a source. But how to access?
That person must have had siblings:
telling a story makes it true, and having no one
care about it makes it disappear.
When my mother and my aunt argue
about what happened, or one of them entirely
forgets a wound, I see I have only
the little I've made myself, and I don't trust it.
Explore the depths and love the difficult, Rilke said.
But when I tell myself to remember
whatever sadness and pain were there, I can't,
the beach glass past tumbled smooth
and opaque from scratches, my childhood
swallowed the way the ocean absorbs
debris, even the occasional ship.

We Saw No Caribou

except on metal signs, the cartooned
antlers ungainly, black against yellow.

Were we not still enough when the heat of day
had dissolved and the animals coolly

made their way into the blue dusk?
We drank their water, ruddled from the rocks,

and shared their air, as clean as absence.
We would have photographed them, of course,

along with the Montmorency Falls, the Île
d'Orleans, notched on memory's belt, accreted.

And if we had beheld caribou, moose—or cougar!—
would the sight have blessed us

like the Shroud of Turin
or simply been allied with one moment,

contained in time by the word *vacation?*
In a Bierstadt painting, they'd be larger

than the Indians, smaller than the sky, part
of the grandeur. Disney would make them

friendly, laughable and safe. In a zoo
we'd say forlorn, circumscribed by fake

rocks and pools. In our photographs
a sheared fur of trees wraps the hills.

Below us the lakes stretch and curl.
Around our bodies an altitude, around

our heads a nimbus. And in the center,
freed of their anchor in God, our eyes

look back at our immanent selves.

Passing

Are teapots art
if sufficiently awkward

or plates
with a poisonous glaze?

I keep dreaming of making things that might, like the beveled
edge of a mirror, compound value:

method antinomic, attitude questioning
result, still sometimes birdshit—

in such dreams I am always responsible
for the distance between burnt umber and brown

the roots concealing themselves
in the pilled wool of my pullover

my eyes a soldered bridge
mute before the questions, *what's it for?*

how long will it last? If irony's passé
shall we bring on beauty, the kind that has absorbed its opposite?

If not why not hovers over
virtuoso, tour de force & trompe l'oeil

but who can know the depth of even one's own heart—
access is guarded by a hard flame.

My ever-breaking promise of bliss:

If it holds water, is it art?

No matter how the poplars hold back the hill

as straight as any trees could be

they sway, as a mountain can appear the only one
or a link in a colossal chain.

One writes in a trance, the other applies Teutonic discipline:

shouldn't it *look* easy?

Let's varnish usefulness for long duty—
Christmas in the tropics—let's festinate
the yellow daisies into bloom, so icy in their blown glass—

trouble

                        squeaks by
pink slip, lazy maid
spoiled hors d'oeuvres

            she's a swamp

the body rusts, ovaries
removed like pokeweed

in the family's way
and in it with the law

she's a trifle with whipped cream
& sulfuric custard

            but sludge ladies
can bake bricklike cakes
                        (we're good at breaking eggs)

so let's let trouble
into our hearts like a string of South Sea pearls

                black, luminous

and raise her as a statue
over all our small affairs

Tale

At a party a woman tells the guests
she's got a tail, and I of course think
she means a *story*, but then she gets up,
and emerging boldly from her skirt, is her tail.

It's mouse gray, and strong, strong enough
for climbing. And oh, on the end it's got a hand,
covered in fur, reaching past her knees when she stands.
She wraps it around her hips when it's not wanted.

By now the others have lost interest,
they're watching basketball on TV—what a sight
she'd be in court, tapping a gavel, writing
a note, and pointing to the plaintiff, all at once.

Where can I get one, I ask, but she shakes
her head: it's nothing you can buy,
it's free to anyone who wants one
and can show they won't abuse it.

But why doesn't everyone, I cry—
and then another thought creeps in: I hardly use
the limbs I have, I should examine her tail for lice.
With sadness in her mien she nods,

yes, you'd think it would be common,
you'd think it would be prized.

Open That Door

Nothing can get through.

Well, maybe some ants: unaware
that what marches into the world
does not always return, ants get in
everywhere, and they know
where they're going.
                    And the rhinoceros:
dynamite packed into the horn
and a long fuse wrapped inside the body,
its tail lit by fiery scent. In recompense
for a lifetime of eating grass,
the blind and shiplike rhino can splinter
that door.
                    But the magpie: incessant
as tropical rain, the black-billed, white-bellied
pica pica's silly with the sound
of its own iridescent cheer, continuous
as stars we can't see shining, so that
someone sitting inside a house while a magpie
pipes outside cannot but eventually,
in irritation and amazement—

Heaven

An ocean liner. The other passengers everyone
   I love or might have loved, and in the center of the ship
a library with mahogany tables. Cats

curled on open periodicals. No fleas.
   Pellegrino in the fountains and Gertrude Stein
lecturing about the art

of being dead. Walks with Mary Shelley.
   Mary, I say, *where's the creature?*
When the new books arrive, we differ

politely over who gets what. But wait—
   with a few improvements this could be
an artist's colony, and with a few more,

my life. I know I am lucky
   to do what I love, but I yearn for time—
time as a river of milk whose blankness stretches

over my body, strong enough to climb
   Mt. Olympus. I'm remembering Norman
on Majorca, Norman who dropped out of Madison Avenue

in the sixties, who let me buy him
   a rare steak for a watercolor of a bullfight.
Me, twenty-two with a backpack and Swiss francs

and Norman, fifty-five, with a wide grin, missing
   teeth. He quoted Marx, and Henry George,
the durability of the means of production is a great

part of its use value; private land enslaves
   the working class. In heaven work and play
will be woven of the same

---

endless silk. And when we sail
   from the shore where busy hands
sew flags and signal

frantically? We'll turn away
   from the rails on this ship
powered by the heat of our souls.

Chicken Scratch

On days like these the sky keeps changing—
lanolin to mouse to cornflower—
the sun a chrysanthemum yolk, my heart,

cooped. The sky like the rest of me
as I pull myself from task to task, a chicken
scratching. I can't marshal the cells

of my body into flocks, nor tell
my neurons to fly. An omelet runs
like the words in a scrambled letter

I've been trying to write. My muse
won't obey: my eyes are wild blackberries,
my feet jellied and monstrous, my sex locked

into its unreliable, delicate shell.
My thoughts go out like chicks on the highway
to find a cornstalk for the Royal Rooster,

but are pillaged by marauders, held
for ransom. Still I hope—how many
things are judged impossible! If

the world is will and idea, will I
tease chickens out of eggs,
even when the King won't pay?

Leave No Trace

How can you not notice
the Russian Olive, its gray-green sneeze of color,
or me here smelling of myrrh? I'm
a sonata played with half the notes.
I like all ten fingers on the keys
and an eye that looks beyond itself
to the woods ten versts away.
                              Of course,
if you were the National Forest, I would not
rub sticks in your vicinity, I'd
muffle the underfoot crackle of leaves,
and even in my ears I would carry
water. But my hands are dusted
with gunpowder.
                              Who built the first house
and when will the last one collapse? The red
room of your head is unfurnished,
mine resembles a Bedouin tent. With the top
open, the piano can be heard everywhere
the cheatgrass is burning. You will be fed milk
and kasha soup, cabbage and potatoes. Blue
bottle flies and my shoes covered with foreign
seeds. I get my license from promising.

Bad News

I demand you return the key
to my mustang because the thought
of you driving to Arizona
with your warm posterior glued to my
lambswool pushed me over: *give it back*
I say, meaning everything you'd fished
from me. I'm a grown woman
and I like change but I prefer not to
erode—think rodere (to gnaw), think
rodent (you). In my country frankness
is raised to new heights. Goats
make the climb in bare feet while raptors
circle overhead. I am happier in the company
of raccoons who wash their hands before they eat.
Imagine the fine hairs of a caterpillar.
When they touch me I am stuck or is it struck,
by the need to know
whether you'd done what you did
out of malevolence or ineptitude.
Though it's too late now for distinctions
between Elmer's and Flicka, between a sand burr
and stockings stolen from a drawer.
Give it back, I say as though speaking into a phone
whose voice answers, *press one for Spanish,*
press two for Dodo, the language of diplomacy.
You speak the tongue of clams. As for me,
I talk the way a tail invites pursuit: come
here, you viridian-eyed rattler, come here.

Beyond Good and Evil

You're standing in your apartment,
the one where you've spent years savoring
the lines of the Mission Oak bed, the thick
Chinese carpet, the calla lilies
in their celadon bowl. You are standing
there and someone with a key lets herself in.
She's unkempt, a wild thing—smeared lipstick,
calloused heels. *How did she get a key?*
You tell her she may stay in the spare room
and she appears to agree: no smoking,
no parties, just slippers on the waxed wood.
Next thing you know, she's in the kitchen
with twenty of her friends, smoking cigars
and listening to Pearl Jam. The lilies have tipped,
the granite's been scratched, and she's got her hand
in your silver, fingering the filigree of the cold meat fork.
You remember Nietzsche, *the high spirits of kindness*
may look like malice. She's been sent
to deliver you: should you kiss her feet?
She embraces error the way frogs walk.
Her hammered beauty doesn't
recognize itself. Didn't Nietzsche make Truth
into Woman, knowing that simple
opposites are malicious in their simplicity?
You wonder what it would be like to hold
a cigarette between middle and first finger,
flick ashes across table linen. It's time,
you tell yourself, to be outside. To wade
through a river of gin in fishing boots,
to breathe deep of tar-soaked air.

Song of the Cook

I chant the pickled alewife, I wallow in surfeit

   plums simmering magenta
   culled & staining
   a backdrop for intrigue

   I excise hearts

I let edges be edges and
where would I be without my thin blade?

Somewhere a woman is washing her hands with wine
on her breath, and elsewhere garlic
heads tumble to a pink tiled floor

My fingers are forks, my tongue is a rose

   herb-snip
   meat-whack
   root-chop

I turn silver spoons into rabbit stew
make quinces my thorny upholstery

O custard apple pudding of applied love
O cider wheedling its sugary tune

how else could the side of beef walk
with the sea urchin roe?

How else could I seize what I see and ride
my bird's-eye maple broom

   into the night sky's steam?

Scrabble

I've learned not to hoard the letters,
not to keep the "u" sidelined,
waiting for a "q,"

not to save the seven-letter word
while hoping for an extra fifty points.
And that it's rarely wise to skip

a turn for the chance to trade in all
one's letters, that I'm much better off
eking out "e's" or "i's"

because I can't bear to think that I'm not
satisfied with my lot,
that I don't have it in me to make do

like my mother after the war, turning
curtains into clothes, boxes
into furniture, weeds into salad.

So the click click of chips of wood
is the sound of someone making words
fabricate serenity, making intellect

administer the feeling of always
wanting more. And the other sounds
you would hear even in a soundproof room:

the low hum of circulation,
the higher hum of the nervous system.
It's not a game of luck, of course,

but memory, and most of all, building,
stacking words like sunwarm bricks
that fit so well I want to stretch out

on top of them and rest,
though not long enough to miss "jackpot"
or "managed," not long enough to miss

the chance to order
my own heart's clamor into seven letters.

Regrets

I regret I sleep so much, that my body
          makes demands I do not refuse. I regret
my thirties, unreasonable as crabgrass,
          and I regret the two vertical lines between
my brows, the manifestation of my anxieties
          which of course I also regret. I regret
the Swiss milk pitcher broken by the neighbor's
          cat and I regret my soft teeth. I regret nights
I stayed awake baking or reading novels
          that changed me only momentarily. I
regret that capitalism is my religion
          and the small red purse I do not use.
I regret lying in the sun as a teenager and
          not putting a safety catch on my grandmother's
brooch. I regret the poisoned dish of lacquered duck
          in 1977, and the squirrel that last year
got caught in a rat trap. I regret the Procrustean
          bed of my job and having no columbine
seeds from the beds by the old library. I regret
          the demise of the streetcar and the perils
of color, and that in my sleep I do not dismantle
          silence. O my Great Lake of Regrets,
my body a floating island—

Thanksgiving

Be grateful for the bad things too, says Rumi.
I'm glad I sit in a room with a thumb-sized wasp.
A gust of warmth might wake it up
to stinging. Of course, I could have been
put stark naked in a barrel stuck with nails
and dragged along by two white horses. Maybe
that will be tomorrow's boon. But now
I'm happy for the bunion on my foot,
and for this gray November day that turns
the trees to angry veins, and for tobacco
with its sturdy grip on friends, their lively coughs.
I'm much obliged as well to mischief I myself
have caused: my petty meanness in the air
like gasoline, my callousness a vinyl cloak.
But most of all, I thank God
for Sloth, the bear who eats my hours
so avidly. How difficult life would be
without you, Sloth, an uphill road of industry.
You make a drowsy wasp of pain.

Marcel at the Station House

If you find yourself being questioned about a crime you did not commit,
resist at all costs the impulse to be helpful.
                                                    —Social psychologist Richard Ofshe

Where were you on the night of July 10?

I am unable to say from what place, from which dream, anything comes.

If you were to commit a crime...

I would prepare the hundred masks that must fit a single face.

You would plan it?

How many persons, cities, or roads does jealousy make us eager to know?
I'd think about details.

Like hair and fibers?

Like *boeuf à la mode*, like water lilies, like Vermeer's *View of Delft*.

You went out to dinner that night?

I observe, I speak with servants, I remember.

But sometimes you do the things you think about?

Nothing is so satisfying as the imagination's rendering of it.

Because you have a bad memory?

Hours go by and I remember the tremors in my thighs.

So how do you...

I like to watch famished rats clawing and biting each other.

Are you kidding?

The day my mother died she took her little Marcel with her.

And how did it feel when you first put your hands around her neck?

A slight ripple, like sipping linden tea or feeling a fingernail trail against a taut stomach.

What was she wearing?

A Fortuny gown, pleated red silk, and diamonds. Red shoes, of course. Everything of those days has perished, but everything was born again.

Did you love her?

I prefer to remain closeted with the little person inside me, hymning the rising sun. He would make me happier than she.

There's a lot of evidence. We have a lot of evidence. We have your hair.

I'd curl it to face the photographer. I'd wear my velvet jacket, and the apple trees would expose their broad petals of white.

You were nervous? You stuffed the body in the trunk?

No, I would have laid it on an old satin coverlet, after which I would have consoled myself, if I felt well enough, by walking along the avenues. I would have taken my walking stick, I would have sung at the top of my voice. I would have taken a few grams of Veronal.

Are you sorry?

Ars longa, vita brevis.

Which means?

I am acquainted with sin, in one form or another. Dostoevsky writes about murder, but did he commit it? Laclos was the best of husbands.

But you?

I don't invent things. I've become braver, thinking of my journey into the self like climbing down a well without a rope.

You used a rope?

O! The trinity of braided strands, the coarse erotic fibers.

I'd like to try a polygraph, if that's all right with you.

The Statues

One morning the people of the capital awoke to dozens of bronze statues: in front of parliament, a horse and rider both the size of Great Danes; behind the concert hall, a waif in a tutu on a tree stump playing a huge violin. In the library lobby, a creature with a low forehead, protruding teeth, and hairless paws, a cross between a cocker spaniel and a warthog. The Queen, it seems, had cast enlargements of the miniatures on her dressing table.

It was rumored that the statues contained secret cameras, and that a royal eavesdropper had been appointed to monitor conversations. In protest the citizens tied balloons to hats and gave the warthog sunglasses; they placed mounds of chestnuts below the rear ends of horses.

The philosophers found a lesson in irony. The doctors wondered if the Queen was senile. The artists, of course, hurt most deeply. Surrounded by such ugliness, how could they teach beauty? But the people learned to live with the statues—the Queen had, after all, put bread on their plates— although there was a precipitous rise in both melancholia and glaucoma. It was like living with the sound of a cracking whip. Did the Queen know, the people wondered, that when she died, the statues would be melted into a coffin for her, with her body like a ladybug inside a tuna fish can? It would take an entire regiment to carry the bier.

Vice

Their Mormon parents out of town,
   the neighbors' kids are partying.
      Without alcohol, tobacco, sex or drugs?

Without religion, at their age I was "good."
   Or was it spineless? How hard it is
      to navigate the laws of God and man!

What's your porn name, asked my friend John:
   Your childhood pet plus the street you lived on
      then. He's Darby (dog) Howard (road).

The neighbors' kids don't have pets,
   they'll be bishops and brokers like their folks.
      It's quiet now, are they counting tithes

or forging Temple Recommends?
   Vice must have variety, said Byron.
      I'm thinking about my wicked streak,

the way I like to judge. And about
   the evangelist's son I went to college with,
      who stole lines from Gary Snyder:

"I pull out your blouse,
   warm my cold hands on your breasts."
      Today he has endowed the school;

his Christian broadcasts warn
   against the scourge of sexuality.
      Not the lapse so long ago,

but what he stands for now
   is why I've disavowed my alma mater,
      or to be honest, have been meaning to:

To Whom It May Concern:
    you've taken his two million,
        from me you'll get two cents!

I know it's hard to change,
    to make one's acts reflect one's heart.
        Mine only sometimes synchronize.

I pray he sees the light. But no—
    I lie—I really hope he'll be discovered
        using church funds for a kiddie porno ring.

My letter sits unmailed
    while I weigh the road to hell.
        Sincerely, Muki Charles.

The Philosopher's Name Was Misspelled Everywhere

Man is the cruelest animal. She wanted to sleep with the philosopher, she wanted to feel the warmth of his back against her chest. Some people had trouble with the consonants, others reversed the vowels. He made her think— that was his gift. She wanted to name a restaurant after him, the offerings cued to his epigrams: Bellwether Pie, Christian Vice Pudding. *The abdomen is the reason why man does not easily take himself for a god,* he had said. She was always hungry but she knew words wouldn't feed her or save the Tutsis in Rwanda. When she thought of genocide, she wished she could lose her appetite. Of course he'd been dead longer than the million Tutsis who had been macheted into pieces. A low-tech war. Unimaginable, she would have said, a hundred years after the philosopher's wisdom: the savage appetites of ordinary people turned to killers turned back to ordinary people.

Story of a Marriage

A purple gray sky resembles ashes of roses.

Inside the house ceilings sag.

She is one farmer who talks to dairy cows inventively.

He wears ear muffs even when he feeds the pigs.

The Other Woman vomits regularly.

When the sap evaporates, grit seeps under their eyelids.

Her imagination is a hair shirt, his has holes.

Texas clay sinks around their foundation.

The heel of his shoe, the barometer of her face—are not rubber.

Near the end her skin blooms with violet rugosa.

Like a hemlock he loses his needles.

They keep the one key that doesn't work.

Baltimore

My honeyed city of slurred syllables—

Southern city of planters who wanted to secede.

City of glassphalt, of lead paint.

City where I rooted, and neighbors watered me.

Pigtown city
          of screenpainters, pipe fitters, silver chasers.

City of strawberries and sad-eyed horses, Arabers.

Maiden-aunt to the city of Brotherly Love.

Old Bay—Crab city
               of spice and water

taxis, formstone city with no one strolling the streets.

Leafy green Olmsted city
                    gutted.

Frederick Douglass's city
               of libraries closed, lymphoma.

Tooth-shaped city of Red Light Running,

city of Billie and Babe.

               Of my turn from *me* to *we*, my civic self.

City I loved for twenty years, and have left

forever, as surely as the siren—

too late, too soon—

sounds on Mondays at one.

My Secret Life

That gent in Victoria's England who screwed,
frigged and gamahuched his days
as though they were feathers
and sex were air,
wrote a book I loved reading.

My own history is represented by lacunae:
license, or *pillow*, a word
I can't remember ever writing,
although I had a childhood square
of ticking that smelled of skin

and made every corner safe for sleep.
Whose stripes met at rough seams,
like the ocean and the shore,
the present and the past, thinking
and doing. If I had done more,

my secret life might be eleven volumes
instead of a hundred words, absence
leading only to more thinking...
which *is* a kind of doing—
like nuns in cloisters making peace—

only thinking's faster, and doing
leaves some residue. *Things work out,*
writes a friend, a platitude
that calls to mind creamy worms
driving their way out of chestnuts.

I admire their expulsive force.
But I've been happy
swimming in my pool, in water green
as the eyes of an odalisque.
The thought of drowning is a century away.

Seven Types of Ambiguity

in the apricot pit of my longing
       two hundred fruit-biting purple finches

         light of day kills a porcupine mid-road
whose flesh tastes better than beaver

           you are a spruce beetle eating long curved tunnels
            through my inner bark

an unhunted lion at noon
      and between us a saucer of milk, to be sipped or tossed away

        what you carry, hooked into your skin like chiggers
           is suffocated or reproduces

a copse of twinberry bushes, berries large and luscious black
       bitter and unpalatable

           pink granite—canyons and canyons of it
            beside this incident of us

I Want but Can't Remember

the name of that wax inside a sperm whale
that's used to fix perfume; it sounds like *amber,*
amber, amber, which delivers through turbid fog
the Baltic Sea, fossils with zeros,
the ring my mother wears,
colored like a cat's iris flecked with black,
along with the summer she bought it
in Austria the year I turned seven
when my hair was still dark and thick.
I was photographed next to the car,
the Alps in the background.
At that mountain pass gift shop,
the first time I remember
coveting something—an amber necklace—
that I didn't ask for or even admire out loud
as if I understood it can be fine
to want something and not get it,
that wanting is a secret hymn, a way
to pass the hour shielded from the glaring sun
and tortuous mountain roads,
that you become part of the wanting
like a wasp caught in resin,
buried in sand and waiting to be found.

Reading the Menu

This is my favorite
part of the meal,

she says, looking
up at her friend with eyes

bright as coins in water.
It's when the artichokes

are so young they can be
eaten raw; when the coriander-

rubbed tuna with tamari
vinaigrette is medium-

rare; when the Kiwano melon
lemon ice lasts; and when

the Barolo's bloom waits
to fill the air with berry

and leather.

       At this moment
the past is a small mouse

twinkling around the edges
of the room, the future sits

like a pasha on his throne
and the present's diaphanous

peignoir of words
makes them forget

what hasn't been offered.

Pink Parken

The menu-writer mishears the chef
and it's included on the menu. Three years running,
catering clients don't question it,
so it lives on lists of mixed crudités,
this root, this leaf, this sprout, this flowering
head. Cousin to endive?
Sister to radicchio? No, this is better,
best of all: crisp, sweet, sharp, bitter, soft,
bright, ruffled, flat, round, magenta or rose,
from Chile, Mexico, Thailand, Hawaii, Holland
or cultivated in a San Diego greenhouse and sold
at Dean & DeLuca.
I'd like to be a hungry guest at those weddings
to stand over the vegetable platter and see it
glow like a western sunset,
nestled between the white asparagus and purple potatoes.
O pink parken, I love you more
than anything I could actually put in my mouth—
I want to be fed by your absence!

I am peeling four pink grapefruit

to make sorbet with Campari, for a party,
removing the bitter white pith,
but I am also eating so many sweet globules
that the I who is doing the work
is clearly not the I swallowing the fruit.
Soon there's no hope of sorbet for six,
only enough for two; one of us
boils the rind and sugar into syrup,
freezes the small mound into dessert.

The self who hops to conclusions
like popcorn, who falls in love on the basis
of a bare arm, the self always
drunk with the pleasure at hand, shares a body
with the woman who has been true to one man,
who even at midnight when the other I wants
only to roll into bed, is reaching for chocolate and eggs,
melting and separating, envisioning the faces
of her guests at the first mouthful of mousse,
dark as the heart of a faithless wife.

Graphology

Whenever she met someone, she secretly analyzed their handwriting. She wondered if these insights were illicitly gained, like wiretapping, but reasoned that graphology was merely close attention to the person without the distraction of interaction. Each element of the psyche had its equivalent mark on paper: the dominant upper zone of one friend indicated spirituality, the crowded letters of another, greed.

Every so often she analyzed her own handwriting. She trained herself to write in the way she wanted to be read: her capital "I" was simple and direct, her small "d" showed creativity without affectation, her spacing suggested generosity and good will, with a sense of social boundaries. At one point she saw her lower zone getting smaller and she made an effort to be more sensuous.

Another time she noticed that the distance between her lines had increased, indicating isolation. Someone she loved was slipping away from her, like a fish in a stream of water. But she did not know, until she saw her splayed fingers, that she had let the fish go.

Avatar

She thought of her libido as a bird
in the house, blue-feathered,
with a spun sugar beak. What it lived on
was a mystery, although the house
smelled of bitter almonds, and when it rained
the walls were sticky with syrup.
In the attic it beat its wings against
the glass of the one tiny window.

No one could see it
unless they happened to be staring
in, with binoculars. As far as she could tell,

no one ever did, although some people
are like cats when it comes to birds. She herself
grew whiskers from thinking about it.

View of Utrecht

It's over,   she thinks, feeling her psyche
crust,   at last seeing
through   the far end of the telescope,
as though   the year were a Dutch landscape,
the canal   only visible
the moment   before someone stumbles
into the water.   That won't happen now
because it's been   glazed
like a window,   made hard
to re-enter.   Maybe her doppelgänger
had lived it,   had marveled
at the tremor   of a bird breaking
out of an egg,   then had the sense
to twist the sick   bird's neck.

Someday, perhaps,   when a pair
of medical students   is dissecting
her cadaver,   they'll come upon
a curious layer,   a ring
crenelated   like castle walls.
Will they lift it   with forceps and guess
the weather   she withstood that year,
how much   blue wind.

On Melancholy

For a dark space where water beads and trickles
    down stone walls—
        every sound amplified,
            centipedes darting—

for this, like stars

    I have left metallic light of day.

    Unforgivable: to have forsaken light

        chosen this.

        In the middle of the road joy had been small,
          overlooked, like seeds of fragrant
             white phlox.

So now the soul's muzzled,

      strung on the felly of a wheel
    that's turning. It begins, it's begun: the sodden

           wormy burrowing.

Divine Plan: Eastern State Penitentiary

Ruins now,
        in a cherry orchard
                on a hill above the city—

    white-washed cells
        around a central observation point: a divine plan

      by the Friends of Philadelphia in 1820.

It would, said the Friends, *counter the promiscuity of the gaol*
    with its alcohol, its garnish, its dishonest
             mingling.

   Counter the chain gang,
           the sport of the vicious working in public,
                not punish bodies

          but reform souls.

        No more stocks, pillories, tortures.

        Think monastery—inmates
      asked only to pray
    each in his own quiet cell, skylit, windowless, his own voice
                  echoing.

       Think *penitent*, from Latin, to be sorry.

    If you go see it,
if you walk the deserted corridors, place yourself in the

mid-point of the starfish
        you are the guard watching all the arms
        with a clever system of mirrors.

But if the prisoner,

your food is given to you through a slot in the sealed door,
you have no work, no book except the Bible.

You do not see a human face or hear a human voice *for years*.

Complete and austere,

secret from the clatter of the city.

Thick inside walls, your punishment acts deeply
on your heart,
on the soft fibers of your brain.

Its radiant form, its gossamer sticky web—
the seed of experiment—
reproduced
like bindweed, like staph

with you, this very moment its object.

Though you have committed no crime,

though you are not imprisoned

isolated

or surveyed.

You can sleep soundly.

A Girl of the Streets

Look at the birds of the air: they neither sow nor reap nor gather into barns, and yet your heavenly Father feeds them. Are you not of more value than they?
                                        —Matthew 6:26

O Maggie

the tall buildings closed like lips
a sparrow teeters on a bridge

your sweet coat   *a little pale thing with no spirit*

                    making collars and cuffs
                    not making ends meet

winter and raining, what small bird your soft palm

          the city a river your shoes cobblestones

girl of the painted cohorts   *a figure of a girl*

          lights of the avenues as if from impossible distance

in torn and greasy garments, a huge man
                    small bleared eyes
               brown teeth under a grizzled mustache
                    dripping beer

                    because it is bitter, because it is his heart

     bird on the bridge

shoved into the water   couldn't

          a tick of claws on a rail

                    what the water sang

59

The Art of the Novel

In 1790 a woman could die by falling
for her guardian who happens to be a priest

or a man who is penniless. *A Simple Story.*
Ruined. As if a woman were a building and love

centuries of bad weather. *A mirror carried on a highway,*
said Stendhal, and in the case of Emma Bovary

or Lily Bart, a highway to hell, with me riding shotgun.
Did I like the relentless bleakness because Emma's not

me, or because she could be me? Years spent in a haze
of fiction, living through characters, writing about them,

looking for loopholes in cloth woven tight.
Perhaps nothing's changed, love is still fatal,

except today she starts her own company.
But I've had it with this form of desire, this

continuous dream: I can't read in the past tense,
those surprising but inevitable endings. So farewell, Tess,

Moll, and Clarissa; Miss Bennett and Miss Milner;
Isabel and Scarlett. And for the record, novel,

I abandon you—you who are, Lukács said,
the epic of a world abandoned by God,

you who made my world bigger and kept me on the beltway,
life transformed into destiny. My odometer's clicked

past the point of counting. I now prefer footpaths, or no paths,
and thickly wooded country, the moon.

Night Writing

Moon full

    and she is gripped
by the thought that what she desires is there—
more than the moon?

        like the moon?

           as the moon?

Her heart fills

    so soft and low in the sky
she could reach out and haul it in
and almost does

then it floats higher

        just beyond her

and on the fourth night she weeps

because

    seeing it has passed

    shrinking

she can't remember what it felt like

    to be within its light.

Catamenia

How this rhythm bubbles
like a hidden spring, to echo

the one mad tongue
the body knows by heart and speaks

as a penitent in solitary, lucid
in a cell not of its own making.

How these leaves of blood and tissue fall
from the womb—swollen as a night

of dreaming—into autumn.

Dear One

Between us a city of monuments
flitting roof to roof.

High above the street I write to bring you near,
or rather, to find the best distance between us.

I drink but cannot slake my thirst.

The milky white chills the center.

Icicles could break in this cloister where blood oranges grow,
and no one would know—
to the street only the wind carrying scent.

Although it may sound like bells, this is not a love letter.

                              Are you listening?

I am thinking of the timbre of breath
                              and absence,
of what cannot be said, how the best whole is in the numinous clouds.

Language a wood for thought, wrote Susan, and today

I want to dovetail perfectly cut
balsam and watch it float downriver,

watch something unnamable drift away, until

flowing water carries it to you.

The Tunnel

Visiting the town where she grew up
she sees they'd erected a new
footbridge over the railroad tracks,

and bricked the old tunnel shut. The tunnel
through which everyday she had walked
to school, through urine and broken glass.

Children routinely smashed the lights
and in the afternoons threw dead birds
at her. The occasional bottle. Was it

her superior sniff that provoked them?
The other way home longer, less
interesting, the tunnel open in her memory and

perhaps those who had taunted her.
Sweet revenge to imagine them supermarket
clerks in that same town, days beginning

with a cigarette, ending with TV.
It reminds her of a certain *Twilight
Zone* episode: travelers in a hotel

in nineteenth-century England
return from an outing to new wallpaper,
clerks pretending not to know them.

Skies change, souls don't, Horace said,
although she hopes it isn't true.
Maybe she was just lucky to get out,

imagination no system of justice
and transport. In a dream she has to choose

between two hands: the first a full set of Tarot
cards decorated with clawed dinosaurs:
Archaeopteryx, Velociraptor, Megaraptor.

The second holds a blue U.S. passport,
green cash tucked into its pages. These would
take her anywhere, and she's always

been afraid of birds. Salmonellosis, chicken
pox. How did the birds get out
of the tunnel? Those vandals ringing

up chickens. Dinosaurs eventually
turned into birds, but she doesn't
have millions of years.

Parabola

In these mountains it's a ghost, the wind.
How did it end on earth?
Some avalanche of snow, or drought—

No. It died in its bed
like those in the vestibule of hell
whose sin was being small of heart,

undecided. Deeper down, there's a circle
for greed and gluttony. The old cat howls for
water, for food, more so—in its twenty years,

it has only learned to be more so. Can I
be saved from such intensity or should I pray
for it. Good deeds replace faith—and in

their absence, wind. The plucked dry and scentless
wild mint, the yarrow brittle and colorless.
Not even white. Less so. A photograph

of myself at one, standing crazed in my crib,
clinging to its bars with one wide eye larger
than the other, *more so*. My mother's fear

and my father's stubbornness. The cat's clinging,
charming in youth, now a nuisance on wobbly
legs. Always the disproportion, pressing toward

something, somewhere, or being pushed.
Perhaps even the apex is willed. Rare
and troublesome winds are named: *föhn, sirocco,*

harmattan. The people who live with them
get headaches, ions drawing out every last
reserve of sanity. Mouthfuls of sand.

At thirty knots, umbrellas are destroyed,
a body's airborne at one hundred. Plagues
of locusts, monsoons, catastrophic Coriolis

force. Our daily mountain–valley wind moves
only as fast as I can run, aspens
shiver in its ten-knot thrall. It's no excuse

for bad behavior. Cool and warm, climb and dip,
sunrise and sunset swapping sides, its rhythms
are like tides. And any sound caught

is mangled or disappears—

Channel

after Henry Vaughan

Water

       you are, not were nor will be—

           as cataracts & creeks, as river brown as trout,
               as kidney and as skin.

                  Water you *are*, not were
                                nor will be

               rolling ocean green or

quiet

       without wind enough to twirl the one red leaf.

                  What channel does my soul seek?

This—

       snow melting from trees like rain, a clean rinsing,
          a quickness the sun kissed—

       and this—salt desert water swollen with birds feasting
            on brine flies feasting on algae—

            and this—siphoned through sulfurous rock, glacier
               old as amaranth.

                    I stray and roam.

To be useful, to be clear—

Acknowledgments

—the salad dressing spilt on my neat blouse in the Flying Tiger of our emigration

—my second language, that pool of dolphins and sharks, and my first, from which I learned the price of a pot of lentils, greater than emeralds, when one is hungry in the desert

—patriarchy, whose brocade of twisted threads comes from "badger" and "spike"

—books and their authors not named herein, and the marking of literary debt—like distinguishing rain drops while swimming in a lake

—the house on Choke Cherry Lane that, shortly after it was built, slid down the canyon

—the terrapin: live a long time or make excellent soup

—friends who help me find the difference between "lied" and *"lied"*

Acknowledgments

The author wishes to thank the editors of the following journals and anthologies, in which versions of these poems have appeared:

Antioch Review: "Leave No Trace"
Beloit Poetry Journal: "I See," "Reading the Menu," "Thanksgiving"
Canary River Review: "Between the Lines"
Chelsea: "Vice"
Crab Orchard Review: "Baltimore"
CrossConnect: "Catamenia," "Divine Plan," Passing"
Exquisite Corpse: "Song of the Cook," "Bad News," "trouble"
Gargoyle: "Fruit"
Gettysburg Review: "Beyond Good and Evil," "White"
Harvard Review: "Open That Door"
Kenyon Review: "In the Garden," "Reading Henry Fowler's *Modern English Usage*
   in Salt Lake in November"
Luna: "Night Writing," "Heloise to Abelard"
New Republic: "Channel"
New Zoo Poetry Review: "A Girl of the Streets"
Paris Review: "Wonders of the Invisible World," "Marcel at the Station House"
Parnassus: "We Saw No Caribou"
Ploughshares: "A Minor Riot at the Mint," "Graphology," "The Philosopher's Name Was
   Misspelled Everywhere," "The Statues"
Poetry Daily: "I am peeling four pink grapefruit," "We Saw No Caribou," "Reading the Menu"
Poets of the New Century: "Wonders of the Invisible World," "Story of a Marriage,"
   "I am peeling four pink grapefruit"
Prairie Schooner: "Tale"
Quarterly West: "Dear One," *"Seven Types of Ambiguity"*
Shenandoah: "I am peeling four pink grapefruit," "I Want but Can't Remember," "Scrabble,"
   "My Secret Life," "Chicken Scratch"
Southern Review: "Wave" "Heaven," *"The Art of the Novel"*
Tar River Poetry: "Pink Parken"
Two Rivers: "Story of a Marriage"
Verse Daily: "I See" "Heaven"
Virginia Quarterly Review: "On Melancholy," "The Tunnel"
Women's Review of Books: "Avatar," "View of Utrecht"

"Welcome, Reader," "Marcel at the Station House," and "Divine Plan" were awarded the Campbell Corner Poetry Prize for 2002. Another group of these poems was honored with the 1998 Robert Winner Award from the Poetry Society of America. Grateful thanks also to the judges of these awards.